Burby, Liza
Sheryl Swoopes

2/99 "Rosen Preview $12.95

DEMCO

Making Their Mark: Women in Sports™

Sheryl Swoopes
All-Star Basketball Player

Liza N. Burby

The Rosen Publishing Group's
PowerKids Press™
New York

Published in 1997 by The Rosen Publishing Group, Inc.
29 East 21st Street, New York, NY 10010

First Edition

Book Design: Erin McKenna

Photo Credits: Cover © Susan Ragan/AP Wide World Photos; p. 4 © J. Toposchaner/Archive Photos; p. 7 © REUTERS/Ray Stubblebine/Archive Photos; pp. 8, 16 © REUTERS/Arne Dedert/Archive Photos; p. 11 © AP Wide World Photos; p. 12 © Elise Amendola/AP Wide World Photos; p. 15 © Ed Andrieski/AP Wide World Photos; p. 19 © Alan Singer, HO/AP Wide World Photos; p. 20 © REUTERS/Yannis Behrakis/Archive Photos.

Burby, Liza N.
    Sheryl Swoopes, all-star basketball player / by Liza N. Burby
        p.   cm. — (Making their mark)
    Includes index.
    Summary: Discusses the life and achievements of the record-breaking basketball star whose team won a gold medal in the 1996 Olympic Games.
    ISBN 0-8239-5069-7 (library bound)
    1. Swoopes, Sheryl—Juvenile literature. 2. Basketball Players—United States—Biography—Juvenile literature. [1. Swoopes, Sheryl. 2. Basketball Players. 3. Afro-Americans—Biography. 4. Women—Biography.] I. Title. II. Series: Burby, Liza N. Making their mark.
GV884. 88B87 1997
796.323'092—dc21
[B]
                                  96–54268
                                      CIP
                                        AC

Manufactured in the United States of America

Contents

You Can't Play with Boys

Sheryl Swoopes was born on March 25, 1971, in a small town called Brownsfield in Texas. She lived with her mother and three brothers. When she was seven years old, Sheryl walked onto a basketball court to play a game with her two older brothers. They seemed to be having such a good time that she wanted to play too. But they told her, "You're a girl. You can't play with the boys." Sheryl thought this was unfair. She wanted to prove that she was good enough to play with anybody.

◀ Some people think of basketball as a boys' sport. Sheryl wanted to prove these people wrong.

Never Give Up

Sheryl's mother taught her that no matter how tough things get, she should never give up. So Sheryl kept hanging around basketball courts. When the boys needed another player, they would let her play. Sheryl showed them that she could play as well as they could. The boys played rougher than the girls, but this did not stop Sheryl. She learned how to be a tough player from those games. When she was eight, she joined a girls' team called the Little Dribblers. Sheryl was such a good player that the team couldn't keep up with her!

There weren't many female basketball players when Sheryl was a young girl. Today, many girls look up to Sheryl. ▶

Player of the Year

When Sheryl was in high school, she was the best player on the Brownsfield High School girls' team. She was named Texas Player of the Year when she was in eleventh grade. When she finished high school in 1989, Sheryl got a basketball **scholarship** (SKAH-ler-ship) to the University of Texas. The university had a very good women's basketball team. But after a few days, Sheryl became very **homesick** (HOHM-sik). She moved back home to Brownsfield.

◀ Sheryl always plays her hardest on the court.

Sheryl Sets Basketball Records

Sheryl decided to go to a college closer to home. She went to South Plains Junior College. There she set 28 basketball **records** (REH-kerdz). She was named an All-American player in 1990 and 1991. In 1991, Sheryl went to Texas Tech University. The school did not have a good women's basketball team. But that changed when Sheryl started playing. Within two years, her team, called the Red Raiders, became one of the best teams in the country. Sheryl won many awards.

Wherever she went, Sheryl made a difference ▶ with her excellent basketball playing.

Á Good Year for Sheryl

1993 was Sheryl's best year. Her team won the **championship** (CHAM-pee-un-ship), and Sheryl set nine records. She scored more points than any other woman in the history of the championship games. She was named Outstanding Player of the Year and Most **Valuable** (VAL-yoo-bul) Player. She even broke records set by **professional** (pro-FESH-un-ul) male players like Larry Bird and Bernard King. By the time she finished college, Sheryl had won almost every women's basketball award for 1993.

◀ Sheryl continued to play great basketball while in college.

13

Playing in Europe

Sheryl wanted to play professional basketball. But there were no professional women's basketball teams in the United States. To find a team, Sheryl had to go to Europe. She played for the Basket Bari team in Italy. Sheryl played very well and scored about 23 points each game. But she wasn't happy. Sheryl was far from home, and she missed her family. After three months, Sheryl decided to return to Texas.

Sheryl is happiest when she is playing for her country. ▶

Sheryl Makes the U.S. Team

Sheryl was named Sportswoman of the Year by the Women's Sports Foundation in 1993. But because Sheryl wasn't on a team anymore, she spent the rest of the basketball season working in a bank, speaking on radio shows, and playing games with **amateurs** (AM-a-cherz) at Texas Tech. In 1994, Sheryl made the U.S. Women's National Team. They won a bronze medal in the world championships. Later that year they won the gold medal at the USA Goodwill Games.

◀ Playing on the U.S. Women's National Team was a big step in Sheryl's career.

17

A Special Shoe for Sheryl

Sheryl has a lot of fans. Many of her fans are high school girls. Because of Sheryl, more girls than ever before are playing basketball for their schools. In June 1995, the Kellogg's cereal company asked Sheryl to be in its **commercials** (kuh-MER-shulz). Sheryl also became the first woman ever to have a sneaker named after her. Nike, a sports-shoe company, made Air Swoopes, a basketball sneaker for women.

Sheryl has become a famous woman and basketball player. Here she talks with David Letterman on the ▶ *Late Night with David Letterman* TV show.

Sheryl Goes to the Olympics

In 1996, Sheryl was chosen to play on the U.S. women's basketball team at the Olympics in Atlanta, Georgia. She worked hard to be strong enough to play against teams from other countries. In many ways these teams played as rough as the boys did back when Sheryl was a kid. But Sheryl and her teammates played hard and did well. In August 1996, they won the gold medal. It was a great moment for Sheryl and for women's basketball.

◀ Sheryl worked hard when she played against other countries at the 1996 Olympic Games.

A Basketball Legend

Sheryl's dream of a professional women's basketball **league** (LEEG) in the United States has come true. In the fall of 1996, a women's professional league was formed. It is called the American Basketball League. Sheryl believes that it's time for people to see that basketball is not just a boys' game. She wants young girls to understand that they can enjoy basketball and be really good at it too. Sheryl has become a star and a **legend** (LEH-jend) in women's basketball.

Glossary

amateur (AM-a-cher) An athlete who does not get paid to play a sport.

championship (CHAM-pee-un-ship) A game to see who is the best team or player.

commercial (kuh-MER-shul) A message selling something on television or radio that is played between programs.

homesick (HOHM-sik) When someone misses his or her home and family.

league (LEEG) A group of teams that play against each other in the same sport.

legend (LEH-jend) A person who will always be known for his or her accomplishments.

professional (pro-FESH-un-ul) An athlete who gets paid to play a sport.

record (REH-kerd) The highest score ever reached.

scholarship (SKAH-ler-ship) Money set aside to pay for a student-athlete's education once he or she has agreed to play for that school's team.

valuable (VAL-yoo-bul) When someone is very important to the team.

23

Index